Praise for *FARE-THEE-WELL*

"What a journey of hard-won courage—from darkness toward light, from bondage to liberation. Meyers paints her story with vivid images, giving her life a narrative framework that heals her and her readers."
Reverend Alex McCauslin, l/c chaplain with the Father Fred Foundation

"In these brave poems, Joan Meyers transforms her experience into art. The abuse and the trauma don't win. Joan does. And through her poems, we triumph too because Joan writes us a map that doesn't lead the way through her oppression only but through our own difficulties, even if they may seem insurmountable, as hers did. You'll have to remind yourself to breathe as you read this work, but don't let anything keep you from this remarkable journey."
Patrice Vecchione, author of My Shouting, Shattered, Whispering Voice: A Guide to Writing Poetry & Speaking Your Truth

"I am so happy to have been given the book *Fare-Thee-Well: Rescue Poems for Abused Women*). As a psychologist, I am always looking for ways my clients can be inspired to begin the process of change and healing or reflect on the transformation that has already happened in their lives and celebrate the victory. The poems in this book capture the suffering, shame, despair, and hopelessness many of my clients talk about. The poems also give words to the awakening and 'call to adventure' and 'break from the known to the unknown.' I use Joseph Campbell's heroic journey as a template for building hope and resilience. These poems will be another tool for me to empower my clients. Blessed to have been given this book!"
Denise Buchanan, PhD.

CHAPBOOKS BY JOAN MEYERS

The Andy Wyeth Series:
Andy's Windows—2006

A Trilogy:
Lake Superior Legacy—2006
Shadows—2007
All That Remains—2009

Transcendence—2010

Fare-Thee-Well
Rescue Poems for Abused Women
Copyright © 2024 by Joan Meyers
All world rights reserved.

No part of this book may be reproduced, stored in a retrieval system, or transmitted in any form or by any means electronic, mechanical, photocopying, recording or otherwise, without the prior consent of the publisher.

Readers are encouraged to go to www.MissionPointPress.com to contact the author, or to contact the publisher about how to buy this book in bulk at a discounted rate.

Published by Mission Point Press
2554 Chandler Rd.
Traverse City, MI 49696
(231) 421-9513
www.MissionPointPress.com

Book design by Sarah Meiers

ISBN: 978-1-961302-74-7
Library of Congress Control Number: 2024916442

Printed in the United States of America

FARE-THEE-WELL
RESCUE POEMS FOR ABUSED WOMEN

POEMS BY JOAN MEYERS
ARTWORK BY RON LADD HUFFMAN

MISSION POINT PRESS

Table of Contents

ACKNOWLEDGMENTS vii
IN THE BEGINNING— ix
ABUSEMOBILE x

NIGHT LIGHT 1
  NIGHT LIGHT 3
  INDELIBLE 4
  LITTLE GREEN BIRD 5
  HOUSE OF SILENCE 7
  INTERROGATION SCENE 9
  SOME SMALL COMFORT 11
  37th PARALLEL 13
  WINDING SHEET 14
  DOUBT AND FEAR 16
  THE CLEANSING / MY HOUSE 17
  SECRETS 19
  SECRET LIVES 25
  BELONGING 26
  REVENGE 27

HEADING INTO THE WIND 29
  HEADING INTO THE WIND 31
  ONE OF THESE DAYS 32
  REARRANGEMENT 33
  CHANGE 34
  RIDING THE WAVE 36
  CHANGE OF COMMAND 37

FARE-THEE-WELL 39
  FARE-THEE-WELL 41
  THE ANNOUNCEMENT 42
  WARM BREATH OF THE SUN 43
  FREEDOM / SOARING 44

BIOGRAPHIES 45

Artwork

RON LADD HUFFMAN

FEATHER BLOWER—ink drawing . . . . .Cover
SEERS—oil painting (8x10)* 1
GIRL WITH FLOWERS IN HAIR—ink drawing 6
CROW—oil painting (16x20)* 10
DAYDREAMS—sketch 15
GIRL IN RED DRESS—oil painting (16x20)* 16
POD GIRLS—ink drawing 18
ROUGH SEA—oil painting (16x20)* 29
EMERGENCE—ink drawing 35
FEATHER BLOWER—ink drawing 39

ADRIANA/LORE-DANIA, ITALY

BASTA—digital collage 24

Reproduced in black and white

ACKNOWLEDGMENTS

To my writing teacher, Patrice Vecchione, who gave me the courage to set forth my truths on paper and thus to begin the healing.

To all my dear friends in the writing group (Lisa Meckel, Alice Tao, Marina Romani) who offered warmth and encouragement within a nonjudgmental setting.

To Elaine Weiss Whitman, a treasured friend as well as an expert in the field of abuse, who encouraged me in the creating of this chapbook and served as an advisor.

To Ron Ladd Huffman, my editor-in-chief, Feather Press, who was beside me from beginning to end of five previous chapbooks. His dedication to this task was flawless and the addition of his artwork is the binding thread that makes it all come together.

IN THE BEGINNING—

In the beginning, going back even before the marriage, I had glimpses of the dark side of his personality. Yet I went forward, bound myself to a person who was a "spirit killer." And then could not find the pathway out of a seriously troubled relationship.

These poems are only a sampling of the many written mostly over a five to six year period as I began to see the "light," I bring them together for you and for all the others who took the dark, foreboding path as I did. May you find the courage and the support to disengage at a much faster pace than I, and move on to a healthy, nourishing, and spontaneous life.

The first tiny ray of sunlight came in 2001, when I was thumbing through an *Oprah* magazine and saw in an article a reference to a book called *Ten Poems to Change Your Life* by Roger Housden. There was Mary Oliver's poem, "The Journey," with its opening words: "One day you finally knew what you had to do, and began." I read no further. That poem of transformation stirred me as none other had or could possibly do. I immediately printed up copies of it and sent it to all my friends. But it wasn't there for them. I was the one who needed to receive her message. It was that very day that I began my own journey towards freedom.

It's been a long run, through almost fifty years of bondage! But the required strength grew ever so slowly and eventually it began to spiral in leaps and bounds as happenstance brought just the right people into my life at just the right time. Fantasy gradually became reality until finally and determinedly I stood proudly on my own two feet. May it be a swifter journey for you.

ABUSEMOBILE

Climb aboard the abusemobile
it thrives in the darkness of the night
closed doors and curtains cover up clues
the language projected makes one cower in fright
derogatory words pierce like arrows
aim straight for the heart to wipe out life
one never knows just when it will happen
an unexpected killer without a knife
when daylight appears all's back to normal
nothing's out of place, silence restored
a normal day in spite of the nightmare
you're limp as a pancake
last night you were a "bitch," a "whore"

NIGHT LIGHT

NIGHT LIGHT

In the bleakness of the night
I awake once again
with that heartrending feeling
my eyes spy the narrow band of light
at the very bottom
of the louvered shades
that run across the length
of the bedroom wall
and I think if I can only follow
the path of that light
perhaps it will lead me
to the place I need to be
where the sunlight always shines

A dark painting of Georgia O'Keeffe's
drifts through my despondent mind
somber curtain of grays and blacks
with just a touch of white
memory of a surgery she barely survived
where the only light her mind could perceive
was the size of a pea or a pearl
but that was enough to lead her
through the tunnel
from the valley of death
back into life

INDELIBLE

Coincidence has marked my fate
by causing incidents beyond my control
and thereafter I limp along
like a record with a scratch or a warp
never more the perfect harmony
the smooth completion of even
a single day or night

There's a blight on my spirit
so that it no longer sings or hums along
it cannot soar
I bear it heavily
like oxen bear the yoke
an essential part of me is dead
though the remainder of my body
lives on, longing to be healed
to erase the scar obscured from others
but knowing it can never be
the blight remains, lethal and indelible

LITTLE GREEN BIRD

I AM THE LITTLE GREEN BIRD
SUSPENDED ON A WIRE PERCH
LOCKED INSIDE A WIRE CAGE
NO SEEDS TO NOURISH ME
MY SONG LAYS AT THE BOTTOM OF THE CAGE
IN NEWSPAPER FORMAT
AWAITING ITS DISPOSAL
THE NOTES, THE TRILLS, NEVER TO RISE UP
INTO THE AIR AGAIN
GONE FOREVER, DREAMS OF ESCAPE

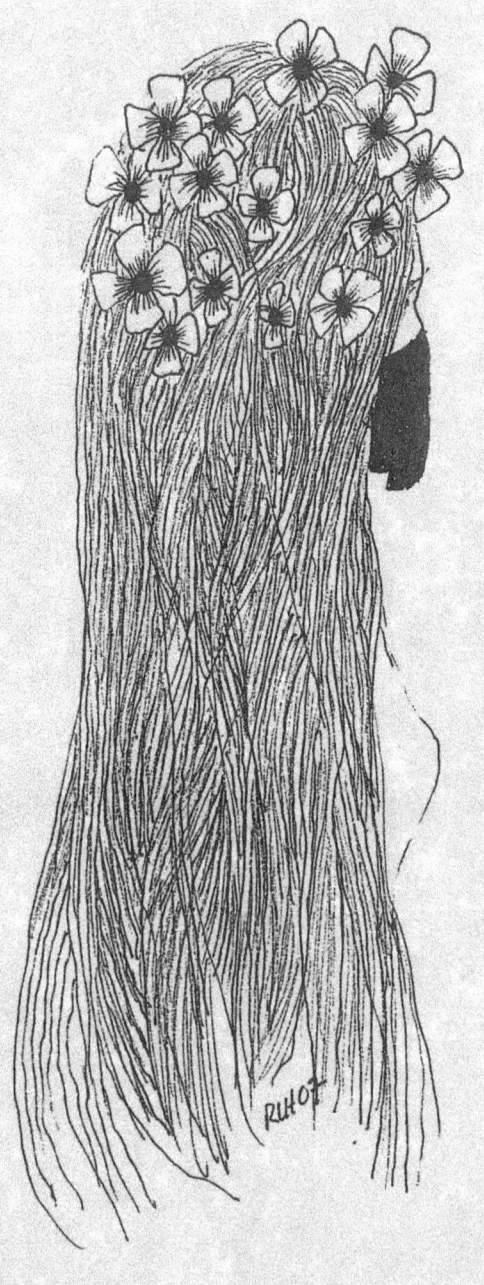

HOUSE OF SILENCE

In the house of silence
no one speaks except to shout
to cancel out the depths of emptiness
ghosts wrap their cloaks around
each and every dusty object
like spiderwebs
and at night they creep against
the shadows of the day

In the house of silence
a single solitary figure
in bedraggled robe and slippers
shuffles back and forth
from room to room
uttering invectives to some unseen spirit
long deceased
shattering the silence

In the house of silence
mirrors turn backwards toward the wall
reflecting only darkness
clocks refuse to tick
their arms move aimlessly about in circles
windows refuse reflection
forever draped in funerary black
and bird songs are kept prisoner outside

In the house of silence
beds are never slept in
blankets create no warmth
spirits slink away to hide
food turns into cardboard
in frozen stomachs
and water from taps runs ever cold

In the house of silence
books without fingerprints
line untouched shelves
music is impervious to the human ear
and paralyzed paintings lose
the power to transcend
nights become days become nights
become weeks become months
become years become decades
become centuries
in this house of silence

INTERROGATION SCENE

In the middle of the night
the bedroom door
is ripped open.
A slumped figure in dark robe
invades the space.
He flicks on the light.
White light jarringly sets
the room ablaze.
Rushing over to the bed
he strips the covers off
the reclining figure
screaming insanities
from a mouth with yellowed
crooked teeth in the midst
of a red face:
"Get out! Get out! Get the fuck out of the bed!"
He shouts it over and over and over again
to a figure that remains mute and immobile.

SOME SMALL COMFORT

Unable to sleep
I stumble from
the restlessness of my bed
groping my way
through the darkness
to the living room
and the cathartic comfort
of the sofa where
my knitting needles
break through
the resounding silence
of the night.

I'm capturing blackbirds,
crows, in squares
locking each one
into separate squares
forcing them into
solitary silence.
How angry with me,
their jailor,
they must be.
I've taken away their voices
split their tongues
denied them their birthright
the chance to squawk and crow
like mad men.

I'm hoping the softness
of the yarns, at least
will appease them.
Each of them equally black
except for one
the one with the albino wing
who resides in a blue square
the color of the heavens.

I can't decide if he's the outcast
or an angel.
I place him in the center
like the Lord God Almighty
the weakest yet
the most powerful.

I've surrounded the crows
with leaves
fall leaves
of a red-orange hue
to set off their blackness
to soften the setting.
Leaves that will be
deserting the tree
leaving the crows
exposed in their cages
each alone and
no voice
with which to
complain.
A cruel punishment.

Poor imprisoned blackbirds.
Perhaps I should
baptize them
give them each a name
make pets of them.
Then I can speak
to each of them
with the confidence
that they'll never
crow back at me.
That's the special blessing.

Funny how they seem
to come alive
these captured crows
in cages
keeping me company—
some small comfort
in the stillness
of a sleepless night.

37th PARALLEL

I hear him breathing in and out
and he's my enemy
sleeping there beside me.
There's a chasm between us
but it's neither wide enough
nor deep enough
like the 37th parallel
the de-militarized zone.
I cover my ears to erase
the sound of his life.
It's either his life
or mine.
Each must follow their own path
or perish.

WINDING SHEET

Each night she climbed into bed
wrapped the sheets cocoon-like
around her body
pulling them over her head
like a winding sheet
creating a deep rift, a canyon
between herself and the other

A half century later
yearning for the love of the one
she slid naked into bed beside
in another town, another room,
she continued to climb into the old bed
wrapping herself in the sheets

Hoping to discover
it was only a bad dream
she would awaken from
to discover instead the man
beyond the deep rift
bound up in a winding sheet
from head to toe

DOUBT AND FEAR

Doubt and fear both wear the same robe
They are my bedmates
Tormenting me before I fall asleep at night
And in the early morning before I am fully awake
Taunting me with messages about what I cannot accomplish

They have large ears, long tails and rotten teeth
And are wrapped in an incredibly ugly robe
They trample over, above and around me
Mumbling monotonously their familiar chants
As I lay trapped under the bed covers

THE CLEANSING

I'm trapped within my own walls
the iron gates do not open
until he vacates
then the walls belong to me once again
and the forest beyond
the birds, the pines, the mountains
all of nature opens to me
I rush about opening doors and windows
letting in the fresh air, the light
letting in life
and breathe in deeply
cherishing the cleansed air

MY HOUSE

The house I live in is so cold
I have to wrap myself in shawls
and blankets of soft fabrics
to feel any warmth

My car is my favorite refuge
it captures heat like a cat's fur
I run to it and revel in its warmth
and that it can carry me away
to places of adventure

Living in my house
is like reaching a dead end
a street that leads no where
I flee from it daily

SECRETS

In childhood, a mark of true friendship
is denoted by the number of secrets you share.
What could be more exciting and bonding
than a friend leaning over to your ear
and whispering:
"I have a secret to tell you.
But you must promise never to tell
another
living
soul!"

Secrets were what kept life
from being one big
bore.
We went in search of them
read books about them
cherished and invented them.
It seemed life itself was
one
big
secret.

And if you were a Catholic
imagine the secrets
exposed under cover of that
suffocating
two-sided wooden box
with shrouded screens
mysteriously opening and closing
to either side—
the "confessional"!

Deep dark oceans full of anguish
earmarked that
torture device
for children and adults alike
more devil than god-like
a terrifying space where
secrets are divulged in whispers
and transgressions erased, eradicated
for the price of a few prayers.

And what of the secrets
hidden deep in the psyche
never to be exposed
under pain of
death
the family secrets
each family holding title to their own assortment.
They are sacrosanct
and never for the
telling.

So many secrets in a family
generations of them
handed down
stored behind closed doors
with multiple metal
locks
each with complicated combinations
as though disclosure would bring certain
death.

I sensed my family's secrets
early on in my childhood
in the passive silence of my dad
the tears of my grandmother
and the anger of my mother.
There was also the anger of my aunt
who long after my grandmother's death
revealed to me in her letters
the heartrending secret
and inevitable
scandal
of her mother's fleeing her homeland
leaving her children behind.

Much of my aunt's
anger
was directed towards my parents.
Why she loved me
I'll never know!
Maybe anger skips a generation?
How vividly I recall her
roughly raking a comb through my
long length of natural curls
as I sat on the edge of
the old metal bathtub.

I felt her iron-handed strength
and hoped she'd never turn
her wrath against me.
She was a powerful woman
all six feet of her.
She uttered curse words like a man
and was known to have
walloped
each of her children soundly
even when they were adults.

I inherited the tradition
of keeping family secrets.
It came quite naturally to me.
It was my birthright.
No surprise, my children
learned to follow suit
and with good reason
learned to keep their bedroom doors
closed
covered their heads with blankets
and went on with their lives
as if "it" never happened—
secrets.

Now in their adult lives
the doors are slowly opening
and bit by bit the secrets
locked up for years in
dark closets
begin to tumble out
no longer in whispers
but in words
spoken aloud
and with revelation
comes release of fear
renewal of hope.

SECRET LIVES

If I could have created the most perfect child
blessed you with only the choicest of attributes
chosen only the most perfect of all males to father you
and nourished you in the most positive of modes
before setting you free
would you then have been assured a fearless life

Why should it surprise me
that you live in fear of the night
night lights are immediately wrenched from the walls
to prevent ghostly shadows
hands in gloves, white gloves dancing across the TV screen
or rubber gloves lurking below sinks in bathrooms or kitchens
elicit fright, hold-over from childhood
panic attacks in the depths of the night

"Momma" she calls me, regardless of my age,
over and over again sending cards extolling my virtues
boxes of them, each one a treasure refusing recycling
she nourishes me taking such delight in doing so
tossing a shawl about my shoulders as we talk about
the secrets we endured when she was a child
together we turn the key, open the door to our most
intimate bond, the secret lives we shared

BELONGING

He thought if he applied handcuffs
and shackled her legs
or tied her to the train tracks
bound her inside a tennis ball
with rubber bands
locked her into a room with
a thousand keys and a thousand locks
he could enforce "belonging"

True "belonging" cannot be held captive
requires no binds, not even silken threads
no rubber bands, locks or keys
it projects a twin, a shadow safety net
even when there is no sun
wears wings to insure its elusiveness
yet has the bonding strength of super glue

REVENGE

Revenge for all those minutes, hours, days, months
and years of cruelty?
no vengeance could ever erase the violations
you wielded with dagger sharp words
plentiful enough to cut an incision
into the heart, directly through its life beat

In the early days, I whimpered like a pup
couldn't believe the crazed words I heard
that leapt like flames from your mouth
climbing higher and higher
until the house caved in
a charred lifeless heap
as if it were a war zone

And I retreated
within my bombed-out shell
dragging my body outside of me

After years and years of injury
a crust formed on the scab of my wounds
emotions seared shut
and tears dried up
replaced with venom
fangs darted out to eradicate your words
and armor encapsulated my once vulnerable body

And after I spewed out my poison
I retreated to a safer stance
wounded still, but without a whimper
scarred for a lifetime
that revenge could neither heal nor reverse

HEADING INTO THE WIND

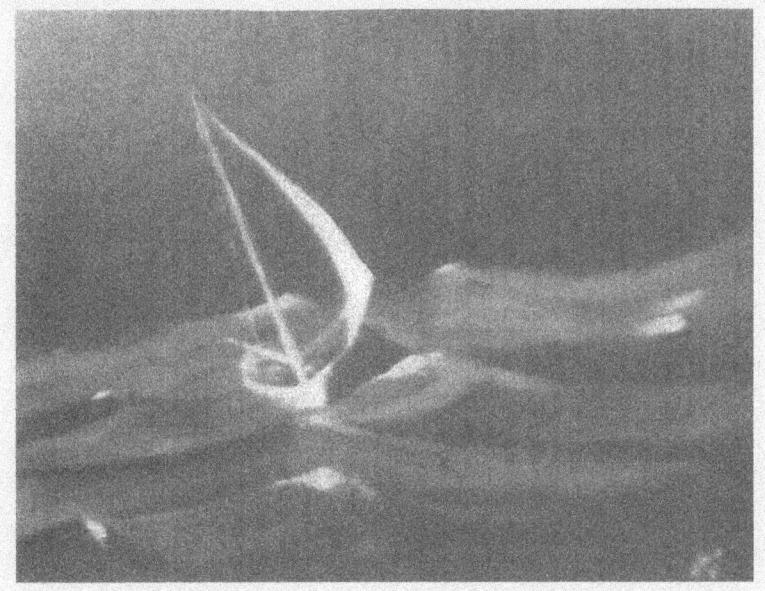

HEADING INTO THE WIND

Prepare yourself, girl
it's the final stretch
you're heading into the wind
put your collar up
fluff up those feathers
expand yourself
gather up all the nerve you ever had
and then some
you can do it, girl

Protect your heart
wear a flak jacket
add a roll of bubble wrap
and tie on some giant sponges
for good measure
for those times when the wind
manages to get the best of you

A helmet for your head
to hold your thoughts together
to keep your mind from exploding
goggles to keep your vision
from blinding you
a set of earplugs
to negate the expletives
you're going to hear along the way

And on your feet
you'll need something
with heavy duty cleats
something that can dig in deep
so you won't lose ground
there's no turning back
this is the big one
the true test
you're heading into the wind
it's the final stretch

ONE OF THESE DAYS

He tells me I better clean up my act
I need some improvement
he's the one who needs improvement
always angry, muttering under his breath
pacing in and out of rooms
opening and closing doors
one after another
doors, dividers, separators

One of these days
the doors will no longer open
one of these days
they'll lock behind him
one of these days
I'll reach beyond this prison
and set myself free

REARRANGEMENT

You no longer elicit fright
your words are empty tomes
recited in a vacuum
delivered to closed ears
ridicule a way of life for you
year after year the threats persisted
they no longer
penetrate my space
like a pistol with duds for bullets

You're puzzled
why I cower not, nor shed tears
protected by an invisible force
far beyond your reach
my strength exceeds yours
you sense it
and being powerless
are now the fearful

CHANGE

Change is moving in on me
like the afternoon breeze
that drifts up from the ocean
gently at first and then
with a more fierce and biting rhythm
altering the tempo
of the tree's branches
they begin to frantically sway
back and forth, up and down
there's a sharp chill in the air
I run for my sweater, my shawl
and head indoors for protection

RIDING THE WAVE

Power is there
waiting in the sidelines
available for you to seize
at any moment
at first a bit fearfully
like a dog whose bark is bigger than his bite
but once you feel even a tinge of it
the teeth are bared a bit brasher
the chest swells, the heart beats stronger
you feel alive maybe for the first time ever
you want to ride this out
like a magnificent ocean wave
the thrill, the exhilaration
after such a long stretch of being limp
just lying there drifting to nowhere

It becomes easier to be in charge
you jump in boldly and call out the rules
stand a bit more erect
fear subsides, takes a back seat
the personality adapts quickly
you're taking control
you're ready to risk it
ready to head out further into the depths
into the great unknown
and there's a smile on your face

CHANGE OF COMMAND

In this household
failure to comply with a dictum
is tantamount to insurrection
and today I am the rebellious one.
Clad in the usual wardrobe
a thread-bare, elbows worn thin bathrobe
his face puffy and flushed
eyes glaring and livid with anger
he enters the kitchen and
with great show of force
crashes his wine glass
down onto the kitchen counter.
Shreds of glass and droplets of wine
spray out into the room and
down onto the floor, drip down
the window pane in rivulets
and leap onto my clothing splattering it
with blood-like speckles of red.

All the bitterness and anger
stuffed layer after layer
for so many desperate years
finally demand emancipation.
Beyond my volition
and with no warning
the words release themselves.
In shock and amazement I hear
a ruthless voice from within me shriek:
"Fat slob! I will never ever
clean up after you again. You
clean up this mess. Then pack your bags
and get out of here! I want you out of my house!"
The exuberance of being in charge
is so new to me, almost thrilling.
I see the look of fear in his eyes.
He appears helpless and defeated
like a wild animal, cornered, trapped.

I step out of the stained clothing
shower, dress and head out of the house.
When I return, chaos has fled.
The kitchen is impeccably clean
and though no mention is made
of the earlier battle, there's been
a change of command.

FARE-THEE-WELL

FARE-THEE-WELL

Stop your ranting and your raving
it isn't you I'm craving
your breath you should be saving
you'll soon see me waving
fare-thee-well

Cling tightly to your technology
heed only your own methodology
cuss the stock market's ups and downs
as your blood pressure zooms out of bounds
fare-thee-well

Heightened senses, over hearing, over smelling
no rest for someone always telling
all the answers, always the need to control
pacing about the house like you're on patrol
fare-thee-well

You don't need another living soul
your aversive personality takes its toll
you can grumble to yourself at each day's start
never ever will you warm another's heart
fare-thee-well

THE ANNOUNCEMENT

The ring fell off my finger
that ill-fated symbol of a marriage
slipped swiftly and easily down
the narrow length of my finger
clanging as it hit the ceramic tile
bounced once and settled into
the far corner of the shower
while I stood there
in my nakedness
not at all surprised
in fact, rather amused
as if I were a casual observer
of someone else's life.

Ever so slowly I leaned down to retrieve it
hesitating at the thought of returning it
to its designated place
though it was not the original
having been replaced long ago
by a modest silver band of more width
such as my grandmother wore
that association being much more pleasant.

The displacement of the ring
was an awakening
the announcement of the end
the bitter end
the grand finale
to a loveless marriage.

WARM BREATH OF THE SUN

I have grown beyond you
and can never turn back
nor is there the desire.
We have always spoken
in different tongues
lived and breathed in separate spaces
you deaf to me and I unable to
relate to your causes and concerns,
eventually unwilling
to make the attempt.
The only thing we shared was a bed.
When you climbed between the sheets
arctic air rushed in to surround you.

Once my feathers felt
the warm breath of the sun
I spread my wings full circle
and with graceful gliding of wings
soared off to freedom.
Uplifted by the heart and soul
of one who believes in me
creativity struggles to give birth
and spontaneity abounds.

FREEDOM

A chance to free the spirit
grab the rope and swing from tree to tree
swing across the river
hop aboard the balloon and rise with the air current
stick my feet within the toe holds of boulders
and conquer that mountain
extend my arm's length into the racing stream
grasp those fairy tale filaments and
weave a life everlasting
then play-act it until it becomes real

SOARING

Fragile little puff of feather
tossed about by the wind
the slightest breeze sends you soaring
you carry my hopes for the future
the new life I am about to enter
I blow gently and set you in motion
watch your determined ascent
the tiniest down of a hatchling
off on a transatlantic flight

BIOGRAPHIES

Joan Meyers has been writing poetry since childhood. A number of her poems have been published in *The Cliffs – Soundings*, Miskwabik Press.

She has created a trilogy of chapbooks, tales of having grown up in an old copper mining community along Lake Superior's shores: *Lake Superior Legacy*, *Shadows*, and *All That Remains*.

Her chapbooks also include: *The Andy Wyeth Series: Andy's Windows* (a collection of poems with reference to the paintings of Andrew Wyeth), and *Transcendence* (poems offering hope and encouragement for troubled minds and spirits). These chapbooks have all been published privately by her personal press, Feather Press.

Joan feels there is a special connection between the world of writing and that of art and enjoys pairing her poems with the work of artist, Ron Huffman.

She also enjoys creating handmade poetry books which include *GRIEF POEMS* and more recently *CAPTURING TRUTHS — A Collection of Favorite Poems by Joan Meyers*.

Her educational background is in literature and mental health. She has worked as a teacher and counselor, helping children and their families deal with a wide variety of problems from severely handicapped children to those facing death.

Joan currently lives in Traverse City, Michigan.

Ron Ladd Huffman (1934–2014) was the creator and editor of Feather Press. He was born in Marlette, Michigan, where he spent much of his life.

Ron studied art at Michigan State University and briefly at Ohio University. His paintings focus for the most part on the natural world with a hint of abstraction.

Ron's artwork (paintings, drawings, lithographs, and photography) are represented in Joan Meyers's poetry chapbooks. He also wrote poetry and his poems have been published in *The Cliffs – Soundings*, Miskwabik Press.

Ron published two collections of his poetry: *Nickels In The Grass* and *raison d'etre* (Feather Press).

He also enjoyed working with his hands, crafting wooden boxes from exotic woods and creating primitive furniture.

www.ingramcontent.com/pod-product-compliance
Lightning Source LLC
Chambersburg PA
CBHW050733010526
44107CB00010B/830